100 Questions and Answers About Police Officers

**Michigan State University
School of Journalism**

Front Edge Publishing, LLC
Canton, Michigan

For more information and further discussion, visit

news.jrn.msu.edu/culturalcompetence/

Cover art and design by
Rick Nease
www.RickNeaseArt.com

Published by
Front Edge Publishing, LLC
42015 Ford Road, Suite 234
Canton, Michigan

Front Edge Publishing specializes in speed and
flexibility in adapting and updating our books. We
can include links to video and other online media. We
offer discounts on bulk purchases for special events,
corporate training, and small groups. We are able to
customize bulk orders by adding corporate or event
logos on the cover and we can include additional pages
inside describing your event or corporation. For more
information about our fast and flexible publishing or
permission to use our materials, please contact Front
Edge Publishing at info@FrontEdgePublishing.com.

Contents

Acknowledgments

These Michigan State University students are authors of this guide. Front row, from left: Erynn Fielder, Anna Liz Nichols, Atchareeya Prasitwongsa, Gina Navaroli and Laina Stebbins. Second row: Julia Kassel, Yu-Ju Hsieh, Teagan LeYanna, Andy K. Hahn, Alexa Seeger and Alexa Alati. Seeger created the charts. Hahn had the idea for the photo illustrations of police equipment.

This guide was proposed and in many ways shaped by Michigan State University Police Department Sergeant Florene McGlothian-Taylor. She was asked to create the department's Inclusion and Anti-Bias Unit, believed to be the first at any university police department in the country. She has spent more than two decades with the department working to engage the community in making the campus better and safer. McGlothian-Taylor brought many of her colleagues to help on the project, visited our classroom and invited the class into the department and for ride-alongs with road patrol officers. She has earned an MSU Police Unit Citation, a Merit Award, and All-University Excellence in Diversity Recognition for her sustained effort toward excellence in diversity. McGlothian-Taylor earned undergraduate and graduate degrees at MSU and was the first African-American female police officer with both the Michigan State University Police Department (1990) and the East Lansing Police Department (1988). She has taught at Grand Valley State University and has presented at a number of national seminars and training conferences. MSU assignments have included road patrol supervisor, special events security coordinator, community team policing program coordinator, records manager and public information officer. McGlothian-Taylor is active in the Lansing Alumnae Chapter of Delta Sigma Theta, a service organization.

Dozens of members of the Michigan State University Police Department helped produce and review the guide, explained special assignments such as the K-9 and Bike Units, and answered questions during ride-a-longs or agreed to be interviewed. They included:

Police Chief and Director: James Dunlap

Chief of Staff: Captain Penny Fischer

Field Services Bureau: Retired Deputy Chief Dave Trexler, Deputy Chief Kelly Roudebush, Captain Doug Monette, Lieutenants Matt Merony, Danial Munford and Chris Rozman, Sergeant Dan Childs and Officers Antonio James, Megan Parviainen, Tim Schutter, Luke Silver and Kristopher Sutherland.

Operations Bureau: Deputy Chief Valerie O'Brien, Lieutenant Shaun Mills, Detective/Lieutenant Andrea Munford, Officer Britten Riggs, Detective James Terrill and Communications and Digital Strategist Sierra Medrano.

Bike Unit: Sergeant Jessica Martin; Officers Zach Rangel, Nicholas Spyke, Eric Acevedo, Ron Kalich and Andrew Rathbun.

K-9 Unit: Sergeants Brandon Murphy and K-9 Loki; Mike Cantrell and K-9 Koda; Shaun Porter and K-9 Justus; Officers Adam Atkinson and K-9s Wolf, Cora and Ozzie; Kim Parviainen and K-9 Bane; Jeff Kurtz and K-9 Jax; and K-9 Training Assistant Nathan Kusler.

Bike and K-9 Unit videos were directed, filmed and produced by Chelsea Aldrich, who also took the photo for the back cover. McGlothian-Taylor was executive producer on both videos and Officer Jamie Fadly advised. Production assistants included Anthony Vogel, Liam Gonzalez and Ibrahim Diallo.

Several other professionals provided guidance for the project. They include:

Andy Lindeman, director of the Mid-Michigan Police Academy at Lansing Community College. Lindeman was a police officer for 30 years with the City of Lansing and DeWitt Township. He has a bachelor's degree in criminal justice/police science from Michigan State University.

David Harvey, deputy director of the International Association of Law Enforcement Standards and Training. He is also program director for the Madonna University Public Safety Leadership Institute and former executive director of the Michigan Commission on Law Enforcement Standards. Prior to that, he was chief of police at Detroit Metro Airport and for Garden City, Michigan.

Lieutenant Terry Dixon is the public information officer with the Grand Rapids (Michigan) Police Department. He earned a bachelor's degree in journalism from the University of West Florida during an enlistment in the U.S. Navy. He was a journalist with two TV stations. Since joining the Grand Rapids Police Department in 1998, he has been a road patrol officer, detective, and prisoner re-entry and state parole liaison. Dixon is vice president of the West Michigan Chapter of the National Organization of Black Law Enforcement Executives (NOBLE).

Mike Jaafar is chief of operations for the Wayne County Sheriff's Office in Michigan. He spent 15 years with the Detroit Police Department, where he was a deputy chief, before joining the sheriff's department. As chief of operations, he oversees operational enforcement of the county's 43 cities and townships. Jaafar is a 2018 graduate of the Federal Bureau of Investigation's 10-week National Academy.

Steve Gonzalez is deputy chief of the East Lansing Police Department. He has worked in the patrol division and the detective bureau. He has been sergeant, lieutenant, and interim captain. Gonzalez has a master's degree in emergency and disaster management and a graduate certificate in executive law enforcement from American Military University. Gonzalez graduated from the Staff and Command program of MSU's School of Criminal Justice. He was also a port security specialist with the U.S. Coast Guard.

David L. Carter, Ph.D., is a professor in the MSU School of Criminal Justice and director of the Intelligence Program. His expertise is in policing issues, violent-crime control, law enforcement intelligence and counterterrorism. A former Kansas City, Missouri, police officer, Carter has trained at the Federal Bureau of Investigation's National Academy, the FBI Law

Enforcement Executive Development Seminar and internationally.

We asked two journalists with experience covering law enforcement to check the guide. One was M.L. Elrick, part of a Detroit Free Press team that won a 2009 Pulitzer Prize. The project led to the resignation and criminal conviction of Detroit Mayor Kwame Kilpatrick. Elrick is the son of a Detroit police officer. He has been an investigative reporter at Fox 2 and WDIV-TV stations in Detroit. He is a Michigan State graduate. The second journalist, Elyssa G. Cherney, worked the overnight shift covering the Chicago Police Department during a period of extreme gun violence in the city. She is a graduate of Northwestern University's Medill School of Journalism.

Brenda Rosenberg is an agent for peace, an organizer and an author. She founded the 10-week Tectonic Leadership program to improve understanding and reduce conflict among Arabs and Jews. She redesigned it to bring law enforcement officers and teenagers together. Rosenberg is Jewish liaison to the Girl Scouts of Southeastern Michigan, a cultural adviser to the FBI and the recipient of more than a dozen local, national and international awards for her interfaith efforts.

The cover photos feature East Lansing Police Officer Jeremy Hamilton, McGlothian-Taylor and Jafaar.

This series enjoys unwavering support from MSU School of Journalism Professor and Director Lucinda Davenport. We also acknowledge two people from her staff, Nicole Bond, for data entry, and Tresa Beardslee, now with the Michigan Department of Transportation, who connected us with the MSU School of Criminal Justice.

Introduction

Local police officers and sheriff's deputies are in the news every day. Their growing responsibilities and the way they do their jobs are under scrutiny like never before. News coverage, politics and cellphones and body-worn cameras make their work more visible than ever, even though police ranks are shrinking.

Like many occupations and cultural groups, police have always been the subject of conjecture and stereotyping. Their encounters with people can come at the most difficult times for people, and police must protect both individuals and the public. The needs of these constituencies can clash. As police and sheriff's departments nationwide try to enhance trust and transparency, they are a good subject for this series, published by the Michigan State University School of Journalism. An earlier guide asked and answered questions about veterans. We thought a guide about police was needed, too.

While law enforcement agents at every level share some values and experiences, this guide focuses on county, local, public safety, campus and tribal officers.

Although state, federal, correctional and conservation officers collaborate closely with local departments, they have different missions. Even among local law enforcement, procedures vary from coast to coast and department to department.

Michigan State University is in an ideal position to create this guide. It was proposed by Sergeant Florene McGlothian-Taylor of the Michigan State University Police Department. Well-staffed and well-trained, the department is right across the street from where journalism classes are taught. Additionally, the university is near city, township and county departments, as well as the Mid-Michigan Police Academy. People in several of these agencies assisted in the development of this guide.

This project benefitted from two new studies. One is the Pew Research Center's "Behind the Badge: What Police Think About Their Jobs." The National Police Research Platform conducted the online survey. It gathered the responses of 7,917 police officers and sheriff's deputies in departments with at least 100 officers. The other study is the Michigan Commission on Law Enforcement Standards' "Fostering Public Trust in Law Enforcement in Michigan."

We hope this guide answers your questions and leads you to conversations with people in departments near you.

Joe Grimm
Series editor
School of Journalism
Michigan State University

Letter from the Chief

The Michigan State University Police Department has held a long tradition of honor, integrity and leadership since 1928. It is a tradition that has proven itself year after year as we develop more relationships with the Michigan State University community and continue to build upon our skills to serve and protect.

Each officer provides a helping hand and a listening ear to connect with Spartans to solve problems and enhance the quality of life on campus.

We embrace the tradition and continue our work in providing a safe environment for Spartans to learn, work and live.

James H. Dunlap
Chief and Director

Michigan State University Police Department history and values

The police force for the Michigan State College was established in 1928 when the first uniformed and armed officer, Donald J. Bremer, began patrolling the college campus. To assist with patrol duties, Officer Bremer received support from student watchmen who were stationed in various buildings across campus. During that time, calls for service were operated by the college telephone operator, who would notify Officer Bremer by turning on white lights mounted on the power house tower whenever police services were needed on campus. In 1934, a second officer was hired to assist Officer Bremer with responding to calls for service.

In 1937, an agreement was made with the City of East Lansing for the East Lansing Police Department Chief of Police to act as a supervisor for the campus police force. Under the East Lansing Police Department administration, the Michigan State College police force utilized three vehicles equipped with one-way radios to monitor the State Police network.

On September 23, 1947, the Michigan State College police force separated from the East Lansing Police Department. Arthur F. Brandstatter was appointed as the Chief of the Michigan State College police force and defined the direction and goals of the department. After gaining independence, the Michigan State College police facility began as a set of quonset huts on the property where the Jack Breslin Student Events Center currently resides. In 1975, a new facility was established on Red Cedar Road, where it still stands today on the campus of Michigan State University.

What was once a one-officer patrol has now grown to a full-service law enforcement agency with over 85 police officers and has become a leader amongst police departments. The vision began in 1928 and lives on with each MSU Police Department employee to provide a safe and friendly environment on the campus of MSU.

Leadership over the years

Arthur F. Brandstatter
September 23, 1947 – 1960

As the first Chief of Police at Michigan State College, Arthur F. Brandstatter established the direction and goals of the organization. Police powers were defined and the organizational presence strengthened, which formulated the concept of public safety on campus. Brandstatter also served as the Director of the School of Police Administration and Public Safety.

Richard O. Bernitt
1960 – 1986

Richard O. Bernitt was known as the guiding force in developing the organization to respond to all public safety needs within the campus community. The years Bernitt served are characterized by the elevation of professional standards and the development of administrators. Bernitt was a firm believer in the need for a college education which, over time, led to the department requiring a minimum of a 4-year degree to serve as a police officer, a requirement that still stands today.

Bruce L. Benson
September 8, 1986 – June 20, 2002
At the direction of Bruce L. Benson, the department adopted the concept of community policing, which created a shift in attitude from neutral policing to close personal involvement between the officers and the members of the community. The department's community policing program became one of the first in the country to be implemented on a college campus.

James H. Dunlap
June 21, 2002 – current
Under James H. Dunlap's administration, the department's commitment to community policing expanded to include all members of the department. Under Dunlap's leadership, the department has continued to grow as one of the largest police departments in the state of Michigan. At his direction, the department has also advanced with technology and resources to assist law enforcement. Innovative units and teams have also been developed, including the Bike Unit, Motor Unit, Inclusion and Anti-Bias Unit, Behavioral Threat Assessment Unit, Digital Forensics and Cyber Crime Unit, Special Victims Unit, and the Ingham Regional Special Response Team. Dunlap has also added a Crime and Intelligence Analyst and a Communications and Digital Strategist to the department.

Today, the MSU Police Department has more than 85 fully sworn law enforcement officers. All have graduated from accredited police academies. Many were trained at the Mid-Michigan Police Academy (14-16 weeks) and certified through the Michigan Commission on Law Enforcement Standards. All officers are also deputized by the Ingham County Sheriff's Department and are responsible for responding to crimes and calls for service on all university property.

The MSU Police Department remains committed to high educational standards. Officers must have at least a bachelor's degree, so they understand the frustrations and rewards of life as college students because they have lived that experience. Not all police departments require college degrees.

Additional training for officers includes the Field Training Program, which teaches new officers about departmental policies and procedures. It lasts about 20 weeks. This also applies to experienced officers hired from other police agencies. Officers receive in-service training throughout the year that provides them further tools with which to serve the community. Advancement opportunities require supplemental training and include special assignments. The department is organized into a Field Services Bureau, Operations Bureau and a Management Services Bureau.

MSU Community Policing features teams of officers within campus neighborhoods with the goal of reducing crime in those areas.

The mission of the Michigan State University Police is to enhance the quality of life on campus by building relationships, strengthening stewardship, and working collaboratively within our diverse community to reduce crime, enforce laws, preserve peace, and provide for a safe environment.

To build relationships and improve police community relations, the MSU Police Department formed an Inclusion and Anti-Bias Unit. The unit is committed to addressing police and community-related issues associated with bias. The unit builds relationships by listening to the university community and finding positive methods to solve issues through communication strategies and training. It employs community outreach and participates in internal and external meetings relating to bias incidents.

This 100-question guide is one step in an effort to explain law enforcement jobs to the public at large and directly correlates to our mission as an agency. Without input from everyone, this book would not have been possible.

To maintain transparency and accountability, the university has a Police Oversight Committee, oversight@police.msu.edu. Officers are trained and equipped for the use of in-car and body-worn cameras, and all official law enforcement duties are recorded per department policy and procedure. The department also requires comprehensive training through its Inclusion and Anti-Bias Unit, yearly in-service training, and takes a trauma-informed approach to sexual assault investigations.

The MSU Police Department advises a commonsense approach to campus safety and mobility. That includes:

- Be aware of surroundings.
- Walk in well-lit areas if possible.
- Walk with others when possible.
- Stay alert and obey signs and signals.

This safety campaign is outlined at movesafe.police. msu.edu.

To report a crime or suspicious activity on campus:

- For emergencies, call 911.
- For non-emergencies, call 517-355-2221.

To submit a tip and be kept anonymous:

- Go to the "Submit Tips" tab on the Michigan State University Police Department's Facebook page.
- Text tips to CRIMES (274637).

The MSU Police Department also broadcasts alerts via the Everbridge platform system by voice, email and SMS text. To subscribe to alerts, go to alert.msu.edu

Rewards and Risks

1 Why do people become police officers and sheriff's deputies?

Reasons include, in order: helping and making a difference, work environment, job stability, health and retirement benefits and salary. These come from a 2013 study by Major Timothy Roufa, chief technology officer with the Florida Highway Patrol. A small, earlier study cited helping, job security, companionship, enforcing laws and fighting crime. This study was by David Lester, chairman of the Department of Criminal Justice at New Jersey's Stockton State College. He surveyed 128 male recruits in California.

2 Are there personal rewards in police work?

Most officers say the work "nearly always or often makes them feel proud." This comes from the Pew Research Center's 2017 report "Behind the Badge: What Police Think About Their Jobs." Overall, 58

How do officers feel about their jobs?

% feeling proud

Whites	58%
Blacks	60%
Hispanics	63%
Rank-and-file officers	57%
Sergeants	59%
Administrators	73%

% feeling fulfilled

Whites	42%
Blacks	45%
Hispanics	47%
Rank-and-file officers	41%
Sergeants	40%
Administrators	54%

% feeling frustrated

Whites	54%
Blacks	41%
Hispanics	47%
Rank-and-file officers	52%
Sergeants	53%
Administrators	43%

% feeling angry

Whites	23%
Blacks	17%
Hispanics	21%
Rank-and-file officers	23%
Sergeants	24%
Administrators	13%

Statistics are taken from the Pew Research Center's 2017 report, "Behind the Badge."

percent reported feeling proud. This was more prevalent among younger officers. About 79 percent said someone in their community had thanked them in the prior month. Forty-two percent said they nearly always or often felt fulfilled doing police work. Most said they felt the public respected them.

3 What are the occupation's major challenges?

About half the officers Pew studied said their jobs frequently frustrated them or made them angry. Reasons included long hours and time away from family. Another was criticism from people who they said do not understand what they do. About two-thirds said someone in the community had verbally abused them in the prior month.

4 How dangerous is law enforcement?

Policing usually shows up around No. 15 on the U.S. Bureau of Labor Statistics' yearly report of most dangerous jobs. The FBI reported that 66 law enforcement officers died of on-duty injuries from felonious incidents in 2016. Fifty-two others died from accidents, including 26 in car accidents, seven in motorcycle accidents and 12 struck by vehicles. The National Law Enforcement Officers Memorial Fund reported that 21 of 41 officers killed in shootings in 2015 were ambushed. That was the highest in more than 20 years. Sixty-four officers were killed in firearms-related incidents in 2016.

5 How does police work affect families?

Mark Bond, professor of criminal justice at American Military University, has written that police officers might take stress home to their families. Long shifts can be disruptive and isolating. There can be cynicism, fear of danger, and tension from a lack of communication. On the positive side, policing is often steady work that brings good benefits and respect in the community. In many families, officers' children are inspired to become officers themselves. Although a high divorce rate is often attributed to law enforcement careers, a Rutgers study of Census data showed the rate is actually slightly lower for officers than it is in the country generally.

6 How much sleep do officers get?

Everyone has different sleep habits, but work schedules can be a challenge for patrol officers. They often work 12-hour shifts to accommodate unpredictable situations that do not wrap up in 8-hour shifts. Shifts from 6 o'clock to 6 o'clock are not usual. This can make for irregular days off. Some officers also work second jobs. Regular 8-hour or 10-hour workdays are more common for administrators.

Training and Certification

7 How much academic education is required?

Educational requirements vary by state and department. Most positions require a high school diploma or GED. For some positions, a bachelor's degree is required. Some departments require all officers to have college degrees. Administrative positions may require advanced degrees.

8 Is police academy training required?

Police academy training is key to becoming an officer. Academies are intense programs that run for months. In addition to training recruits, the academy helps select candidates and helps them decide whether law enforcement is right for them. Candidates must first meet admission requirements. These include education, reading and writing tests, a good driving record and no felony convictions. They must meet vision, hearing and fitness standards. Once accepted, recruits must continue to meet standards or they are dismissed from the academy.

9 What does academy training include?

Academy training includes hundreds of hours of classroom and skills training. Curricula cover criminal law and legal procedures, civil rights, investigations, report writing, traffic control, radio communication and software programs. There is also training in emergency vehicle operations, how to use firearms, self-defense and much more. Skills include psychology, communication, community policing, cultural diversity training and verbal de-escalation. Training can include first-aid, CPR, the use of Automated External Defibrillators, tactical emergency combat care and other first-responder skills.

10 How long does the training take?

States mandate training minimums and most academies far exceed these. In Michigan, for example, the state mandates 594 hours of training. The Mid-Michigan Police Academy does more than 700 hours of training over 17 weeks. Officers must work to maintain certification.

11 How does academy training prepare officers?

Recruits practice on-the-job skills including patrol, responding to calls, interviewing, report writing, accident investigations, self-defense and use of weapons. Interactive simulations teach situational awareness, tactical judgment and appropriate use of force, including firearms.

12 What weapons training is required?

In the academy and throughout their careers, officers train on the safe use of handguns, shotguns, rifles and non-lethal weapons. One aspect is choosing and using weapons, including non-lethal tools, in high-stress situations according to policy and procedures. This includes classroom instruction, range drills and simulations to maintain and sharpen proficiency. Regular recertification will be required.

13 Is police academy training different for men and women?

The training is the same. What differs is that physical testing standards are different for men and women. If anyone fails the entrance standards they are denied admission, and recruits who fail exit standards at the conclusion of the academy do not graduate.

14 What physical assessments must candidates pass to become police?

Tests vary by state and by department. Physical agility tests are required for entry into a police academy or department. There is talk of implementing fitness testing throughout careers, too. Most tests set minimum standards, though superior performance can be a consideration in hiring. The Michigan Commission on Law Enforcement Standards fitness test measures vertical jump, sit-ups, push-ups and a half-mile shuttle run. Requirements vary by sex and age. The New York Police Department has candidates complete six tasks in 4 minutes and 28 seconds that simulate an officer's response to a critical incident.

15 What training happens after the academy?

Once hired, academy graduates receive as much as a year of field training. This is under one-on-one supervision by a field training officer and is specific to the job and community. This is followed by a probationary period. There is in-service training in many areas including use of force, defensive tactics, medical emergencies and new policing methods as issues arise.

16 Who does the training?

Training can come from state police, sheriff's associations, local departments and private industry. Training can include live sessions and webinars.

17 What advanced training is available?

There is training to advance officers' skills, prepare them for new assignments, and that may assist them in qualifying for promotions. Certification and licensing programs vary by state. The International Association of Directors of Law Enforcement Standards and Training designs and delivers training to help professionals improve.

18 Do schools of criminal justice train police?

Colleges and universities offer degrees in criminal justice, but not all are designed to certify law enforcement officers. For example, Michigan State University's School of Criminal Justice does research, studies problems, and teaches crime reduction. Universities may incorporate police academy training into the criminal justice curriculum for those on a law enforcement track.

Structure

19 What are the ranks for police officers?

Ranks mirror those in branches of the military, but vary by department or agency. The top position is usually the chief, chief of police, sheriff or, in some big cities, commissioner. In order, ranks can include deputy chief, assistant chief, commander, major, captain, inspector, lieutenant, sergeant, corporal and officer. Classifications used in law enforcement but not the military include inspector and detective.

20 Do all officers patrol?

According to Pew's 2017 Behind the Badge report, 45 percent of all officers surveyed had patrol responsibilities. Age and sex did not play a significant role in whether an officer was put on patrol. Most police administrators first spent years on patrol. Some specialists, who may be investigators or those with administrative duties, have less patrol experience.

Do officers see themselves more as protectors or enforcers?

How officers see themselves

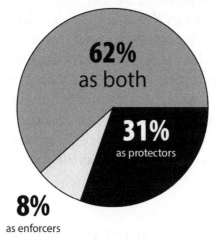

62%
as both

31%
as protectors

8%
as enforcers

How the public sees them

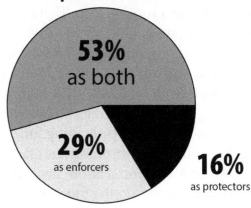

53%
as both

29%
as enforcers

16%
as protectors

Statistics are taken from the Pew Research Center's 2017 report, "Behind the Badge."

21 What is the dispatcher's relationship to police?

Radio dispatchers are the officers' lifeline. They communicate back and forth throughout the patrol shift. Dispatchers relay reports of emergencies and must communicate seamlessly with officers. Dispatchers can also check information, such as whether drivers have criminal records and whether their vehicles are registered. For their safety, officers tell dispatch their location and what they are doing on stops. Dispatchers frequently inquire about the officers' welfare and will dispatch others to check on the status of an officer if they do not get a response. They mutually recognize that their jobs can be grueling.

22 What is a typical day for a road patrol officer?

Road patrol officers say there is no such thing as a typical day or a routine stop. There can be risk in any stop or interaction, on any shift, on any day. Furthermore, circumstances and duties vary from day to day and officer to officer. Generally speaking, shifts begin with "roll call." This is an inspection and a briefing for the incoming shift about outstanding incidents, suspects to be looking for, procedural and legal changes. Patrol work is often solitary and requires communication, instincts and quick adjustments based on the numerous situations an officer encounters. It can include patrolling or monitoring traffic, accident investigations and report writing, foot patrol and handling walk-in complaints. Road officers, now more frequently assigned to patrol alone, may be dispatched to handle calls for service or to assist each other.

23 Is everyone who works for the police department an officer?

No. Civilians perform many vital tasks. Civilians serve in dispatch centers, financial management, administrative assistance, polygraph examinations, records management and data entry. The FBI's Uniform Crime Reporting Program has shown that for every 1,000 people in the United States there are 2.3 sworn officers and one civilian employee. The proportion of civilian employees has been growing. However, one study found they are the first to be laid off.

24 Are there fewer officers on the street at certain times?

To protect safety, police and sheriff's departments do not share their tactics and methods of operation. So, they do not say when staffing is thinner. Without getting specific, they say that deployments and locations depend on the needs expected at certain days and times of day. Special events are a factor, and needs may vary with the season in towns with resorts or universities.

25 What is the difference between police officers and sheriff's deputies?

Both are law enforcement jobs with similar powers and responsibilities, but there are some structural differences. In most states, the sheriff is elected by voters, operates at a county level and oversees the county jail. County sheriffs hire deputies. Police chiefs are hired by cities and other municipalities and are responsible for smaller areas. In places where there is no local police department, the sheriff is responsible for patrols and law enforcement. Sheriff's deputies and police officers work closely on task forces and in other collaborative efforts.

26 Do university police have the same powers as municipal officers?

Yes. University police are certified law enforcement officers and may also be deputized by their county sheriff. They have the same legal powers as neighboring departments. Some also have larger staffs, more training and better equipment.

27 What are public safety officers?

Public safety departments combine police, fire and emergency medical services. Public safety officers typically have licenses and certifications in more than one type of work. The training public safety departments require means they are qualified to help in a wider range of emergencies and can cover a number of roles.

28 What is the role of tribal police?

Jurisdiction on tribal land depends on the offense, location and who the suspect or victim is, according to the U.S. Bureau of Justice Statistics. It may be with federal, state or tribal agencies. Federally recognized tribes, which are sovereign nations, select their own officers. They respond to calls, enforce tribal laws and maintain order. Tribal police can be cross deputized with local, county or state police. This helps apprehension when suspects cross borders. Most tribal police have jurisdiction over misdemeanors and violations of tribal ordinances. Felonies are handled by the Bureau of Indian Affairs Law Enforcement Services or the FBI.

Pay and Hours

29 How much are police paid?

Payscale.com has estimated the annual pay range for police officers nationally as $34,020 to $89,730 with an average of $49,808. Factors include the size of the community, cost of living, local wages and unionization. A 2016 Wall Street Journal analysis of police and sheriff's deputy patrol officers' salaries showed that the national average pay for women was $55,896. That was about 88 percent of the male officers' average of $63,460. In some departments, officers also earn bonuses. Pay is often based on rank. Early in the career, there are automatic pay steps based on experience. After an officer reaches the top of this scale, significant raises might come only with promotions.

30 What kind of benefits such as insurance and pension do officers get?

Benefits depend on the budget and can vary with the location and size of the department. Some include medical and dental insurance and prescription coverage. There are a variety of retirement plans.

Police pensions often begin after 25 years of service with some departments requiring fewer years and some more. In some departments, officers contribute to defined contribution plans. About 3 percent of officers work part-time and receive no benefits.

31 Do police get overtime pay?

Yes. Under the Federal Labor Standards Act, overtime may be based on hours worked beyond the equivalent of 40-hour work weeks or during pay periods lasting as long as 28 days. Time spent in court is part of the workday. Overtime can be voluntary, mandatory or assigned based on rotation. Time-and-one-half is a typical overtime rate of pay. With reduced staffing, some officers work significant amounts of overtime. Some departments offer compensatory time off instead of overtime pay.

32 How are promotions decided?

Qualifications for rising through the ranks are more regimented than in most professions. The process is similar to what happens in the military. Promotions are usually based on interviews, a written test, training received, length of service at earlier positions and performance in those positions. Exams can determine lists that lead to promotions as positions open up and in some departments promotions can bypass the exam process. Generally, chief executive officers determine who gets promoted. Promotions are sometimes governed by state laws that set procedures and policies. In some very large departments, top-ranking officers are considered political appointments. Where there are labor organizations, they may negotiate promotional processes with management.

Special Assignments

33 What kind of training do K-9s and K-9 officers receive?

K-9 officers and their canine counterparts are specialized members of a police or sheriff's department. Being a K-9 officer requires high levels of dedication and flexibility. With a foundation in protection training and obedience, initial training for that canine and the officer can take a month. Training continues after that. Canines can learn to detect narcotics, explosives, weapons, humans or work in crowd control. Many are trained in more than one skill. It can cost $20,000 to buy and train a canine. Dogs may be given the rank K-9 and be assigned badges. They are often included on departmental photo boards and, if killed in the line of duty, receive a law enforcement funeral.

34 Are K-9s assigned to one officer?

Yes. A strong bond between the canine and the K-9 officer is essential. They train together, have the same work schedule and the canine usually lives with the officer and family. Canines might join the force when they are about a year and half old and work five to seven years, depending on health. After retirement, many canines continue to live with their officers' families.

View K-9 unit video at: https://www.youtube.com/watch?v=cCh0Ym4QCoc

35 What is the purpose of horse-mounted policing?

This specialty assignment is used for crowd control. Mounted police work in the city or in rural areas where patrol cars or officers on foot would not be as effective. Equestrian units have also been used in search and rescue, pursuit and traffic control. Because many people like horses, these units can enhance community policing, public relations and morale.

36 What training do officers receive to be on SWAT teams?

Special Weapons and Tactics teams respond to high-risk situations. These include active shooters, apprehending violent suspects, armed and barricaded subjects, and those holding hostages. These incidents require fast responses by heavily armed and highly skilled teams. SWAT teams are often composed of officers from different departments and units who assemble when a crisis arises. The National Tactical Officers Association trains in situational assessment and tactics. These can include negotiating, hostage rescue, ambush awareness and use of equipment including vehicles, shields, non-lethal and advanced weaponry. The teams go by many names. They include Special Response Team, Tactical Response Team, Situational Response Team, Emergency Response Unit or Special Operations Group.

37 What is Swatting?

This is a potentially deadly hoax in which someone falsely reports that a serious crime or dangerous situation is occurring at an address. This can trick heavily armed officers into coming in on unsuspecting people. This has led to some deaths and has serious criminal penalties.

38 What role do local police have in combating cybercrime?

This is an ever-changing challenge. Digital devices are used to commit crimes including theft, fraud, prostitution, trafficking and pornography. Crimes often cross jurisdictions. The Police Executive Research Forum reported in 2014 that local departments were in the early stages of developing responses to prevent and investigate cybercrime. It recommended that local law enforcement join task forces with state and federal agencies and partner with businesses and universities. It also recommended new kinds of hiring and training. The U.S. Secret Service, the FBI and the National White Collar Crime Center have trained thousands of state and local law enforcement officers in fighting cybercrime.

39 What additional training must marine officers have?

Marine deputies and officers start with the same core training and skills needed on land. Additional training can include marine laws and enforcement. Training can cover alcohol use, pollution and noise; watercraft handling, inspection and towing. There can also be lessons in water rescue, swimming, diving and operation of marine radio, sound meters, sonar and underwater drones.

40 What about motorcycle, Segway and bike patrols?

These help in places where cars are less effective, such as shopping malls, campuses, pedestrian walkways, crowded streets and rough terrain. Training and practice focus on navigating traffic and crowds.

41 How do police investigate their own?

Often, internal investigations begin with a complaint. In small departments with complaints involving minor issues, this might be investigated by a supervisor or the chief. Larger departments have a division or section for internal affairs or professional standards. Their responsibilities are to interview the citizen, the officer and witnesses and issue recommendations. Transparency and accountability are key. Investigations can lead to a dismissal of the complaint or a recommendation for discipline up to firing. Another function of the unit is to identify recurring problems. There are also civilian special investigations units. Sometimes, incidents such as shootings by officers are referred to outside agencies to foster public confidence in the final report.

View bike unit video at: https://www.youtube.com/watch?v=YuuYdrAy310

Traffic Stops

The end of this guide has a section that goes into greater depth on traffic stops.

42 What is an officer's procedure in a traffic stop?

First, the officer uses lights and, if necessary, sound to get the driver to stop where it will be safe for the motorist, officer and traffic. This can be on the shoulder of the road or on a side street or parking lot. The officer then tells dispatch the location of the stop and the license plate number of the vehicle. If it seems necessary, the officer might request backup. The officer then approaches the car window, staying behind the driver. The officer looks to see who or what is in the vehicle. Often, officers introduce themselves and ask drivers if they know why they were stopped. The answer can indicate the driver's awareness and state of mind. Officers ask for the driver's license, vehicle registration and proof of insurance. Officers return to the patrol car to run records checks on these. While returning to their patrol car, they watch traffic approaching from the rear and keep an eye on the stopped vehicle.

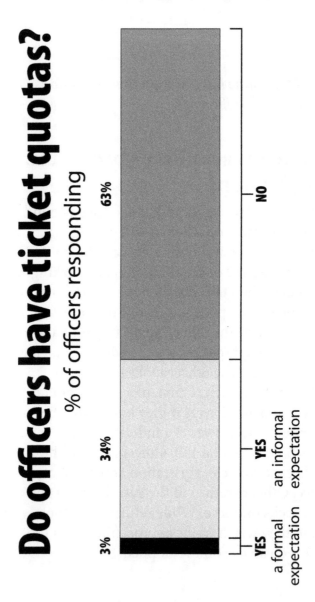

Do officers have ticket quotas?

% of officers responding

3%
YES
a formal
expectation

34%
YES
an informal expectation

63%
NO

Statistics are taken from the Pew Research Center's 2017 report, "Behind the Badge."

43 How much discretion do police officers have when they stop someone?

Every situation is different and officers must act based upon the severity of the violation. The officer may issue either a warning or a ticket. A driver's record may be considered. The officer determines what type of ticket to issue. The ticket sets the path for legal proceedings with the courts. For most civil infractions, officers present their own testimony. Video from in-car or body-worn cameras may be played as well.

44 What happens after I hand over my license?

Several things are going on at once. After speaking with the driver, the officer returns to the patrol vehicle and enters driver's license and registration information into law enforcement databases. This retrieves the driver's history and driving status, outstanding warrants and information about the owner of the vehicle. There might also be radio communication, including a call from dispatch checking on the officer. If technology is slow or there is a problem with the information, this can take time. The officer then returns the driver's license and registration and gives a ticket if one is warranted.

45 Why are there sometimes two patrol cars at a stop?

Staffing today typically puts just one officer in a patrol car. A second officer might be sent as a backup if a stop reveals someone with an outstanding warrant. The assisting officer can also help when people must get out of the car or if a vehicle must be searched. Officers sometimes stop by another patrol car just to see if they can assist.

46 Do departments have monthly ticket "quotas"?

In the 2017 Pew report, 3 percent of officers said they are held accountable for a quota of tickets, citations, arrests or summonses. Thirty-four percent said they have unofficial quotas. Almost two-thirds said they have no quota. In some departments, tickets are measured as one of several performance objectives.

47 Can officers stop drivers outside their jurisdiction?

Jurisdiction is set by states, which often let communities make interjurisdictional agreements. These allow officers to make arrests in neighboring areas. Officers in pursuit of drivers may follow them into other jurisdictions. Officers can also ask for assistance in jurisdictions they enter while conducting investigations.

48 How do officers deal with language or hearing barriers?

This can be a training challenge. Having bilingual officers in the department helps. The International Association of Chiefs of Police recommends officers carry cards with standard requests written in English and other languages. Officers can also use language translation services.

Health

49 What mental health issues do officers have?

The National Institutes of Health published a report on this in 2014. It said a study of 150 officers found that most reported no serious issues. Twenty-four reported Post Traumatic Stress, 19 reported alcohol abuse, and 9 percent reported depression. A Badge of Life study found 108 U.S. officers committed suicide in 2016. In comparison, the National Law Enforcement Officers Memorial Fund found that 64 officers died in shooting incidents in 2016.

50 Do officers have psychological evaluations before joining the force?

The International Association of Chiefs of Police recommends pre-employment psychological evaluations. These can include written tests, computer screenings and interviews. Not all departments use them.

51 Do police receive help with mental issues of their own?

The International Association of Chiefs of Police says this does not always happen. It reported that stigma "prevents both officers from seeking the necessary treatment and leaders from providing it." A 2014 Symposium on Law Enforcement Officer Suicide and Mental Health reported that 46.7 percent of officers studied said they had sought mental-health services. Others declined help, citing concerns about confidentiality and negative career impacts.

52 Are police trained to respond to mental health issues?

Pew reported that 76 percent of officers said working with people having a mental health crisis is important. However, only 46 percent said they had received at least four hours of related training. The need is increasing. Eighty-three percent of 2,400 senior law enforcement officials said the mentally ill population is growing. Nearly two-thirds said time spent on calls involving mental illness was up. The study was by Michael C. Biasotti, a member of the Center for Mental Health Services National Advisory Council and past president of the New York State Association of Chiefs of Police.

53 What is "suicide by cop?"

This is when people provoke a law enforcement officer to use lethal force. People do this by appearing to be an imminent threat to the public or the officers. These incidents are extremely dangerous to police, who do not know the suspect's intentions. The officers involved can suffer Post Traumatic Stress, even if they felt they had no choice.

Police Culture

54 Do police officers take an oath?

It is common for officers to swear to defend the U.S. Constitution, the state constitution and local laws. They often take the Law Enforcement Oath of Honor. It comes from the International Association of Chiefs of Police. It says: "On my honor, I will never betray my badge, my integrity, my character or the public trust. I will always have the courage to hold myself and others accountable for our actions. I will always uphold the Constitution, my community and the agency I serve." Furthermore, there are law enforcement codes of ethics.

55 Do police feel like they are always on duty?

Some officers feel a responsibility to be alert and to respond to any crime in progress, even when off duty. They are more aware of potential dangers than others and remain vigilant. Officers who always feel aware and responsible might feel as though they can never fully let their guard down.

56 Do police officers have to be careful with what they say?

Officers tend to be guarded all the time. On-duty communications can be recorded by body-worn cameras or heard on police radios and are subject to disclosure under Freedom of Information Acts, as are 911 calls. Even off duty, officers still represent the departments they have taken an oath to serve. Some officers have been disciplined for violating codes of conduct with what they have said publicly or posted on social media.

57 What are the dress codes for police?

Dress codes are determined by departmental policy. Police officers and sheriff's deputies may own both a dress uniform and a patrol uniform. While codes can dictate on-the-job attire, departments also adopt appearance and grooming restrictions. Some officers naturally have a personal desire to maintain a crisp, "squared off" look that conveys authority.

58 Are tattoos, jewelry and facial hair restricted?

Guidelines are based on physical safety, order and cleanliness. Some departments allow tattoos anywhere, while other departments allow them only where they are covered by the uniform. Jewelry might be restricted to wedding bands, watches and post-style earrings. Facial hair might be limited to mustaches.

59 Do departments and agencies collaborate or compete?

Collaboration is the norm. Despite television shows or movies that portray turf wars among law enforcement agencies, they usually work together. They train together, have mutual aid agreements, regional response teams and play each other in sports or share other activities. They have a shared culture and support each other.

60 What is "the thin blue line?"

This has several meanings. One is that officers protect society from the chaos of lawlessness. It can also mean that police will close ranks and stick together when challenged or when an officer has died in the line of duty. Sometimes, people refer to "the thinner blue line," meaning that police staffing has declined. Police and sheriff's deputies nationwide express serious concerns about staff reductions. In the 2017 Pew report, 86 percent of police said their department did not have enough officers. The number was 95 percent in departments with 1,000 or more officers.

Use of Force

61 What is "excessive force?"

Let's distinguish between excessive force and deadly force. Law enforcement officers are trained to apply the force necessary to protect the public and themselves. The International Association of Chiefs of Police defines force as pressure used to control a situation or compel compliance. This can range from persuasion to firearm use, often called "lethal force." Excessive force is using more than is necessary. When there is a lethal threat, police may use lethal force. Force does not have to be life-threatening to be excessive.

62 How do officers know how much force to use?

Officers are trained to match the action to the situation. They must first assess the situation. Some departments have guidelines about which action or equipment officers may use in different circumstances. The National Institute of Justice suggests this escalating force continuum:

- Mere presence of the badge, the uniform and calling for assistance

- Talking
- Weaponless "open hand" tactics such as holds or strikes
- Less-lethal force includes batons or rubber bullets, chemical spray, conducted energy devices such as stun guns and Tasers, bean bag guns, and loud, long-range acoustic devices. K-9s can be weapons, too, and are one of the few that can be recalled. Just showing a weapon is a form of less-lethal force.
- Lethal weapons such as guns for situations when there is a serious threat to the officer or someone else

63 How often is excessive force used?

The first major study on police use of force was released in 2018. Of the more than 1 million arrests it examined, fewer than 1 percent involved the use of force, ranging from verbal commands all the way to firearms. Furthermore, of suspects arrested with use-of-force tactics, 61 percent had no reported or observed injuries. Fewer than 2 percent had moderate or severe injuries. One suspect died. The Wake Forest School of Medicine research team was mostly doctors. About half the time, use of force meant holds, joint manipulation, kicks, strikes with fists, knees or elbows, and throwing someone to the ground. Firearms were used in six cases.

Do officers think their department's rules on use of force are restrictive?

The rules are:

too restrictive   **about right**

26%   **73%**

All officers

15%   **84%**

Departments with less than 1,000 officers

37%   **62%**

Departments with more than 1,000 officers

Statistics are taken from the Pew Research Center's 2017 report, "Behind the Badge."

Do officers support the use of tough tactics?

% of officers that agree with the following statements

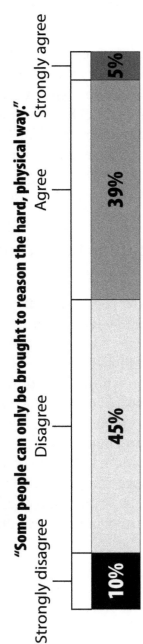

"Some people can only be brought to reason the hard, physical way."

Strongly disagree Disagree Agree Strongly agree

10%   45%   39%   5%

"In certain areas of the city, it is more useful for an officer to be aggressive than to be courteous."

Strongly disagree Disagree Agree Strongly agree

10%   34%   39%   17%

Statistics are taken from the Pew Research Center's 2017 report, "Behind the Badge."

64 How prevalent is police brutality?

Police brutality is using force against citizens that is excessive or unnecessary for the situation. Quantifying it has the same obstacles as measuring excessive force. To begin with, incidents must be reported, which would give one number. Then, departments would investigate to determine whether brutality occurred. This would give another number. Finally, data would have to be compiled nationally.

65 How often does use of force by police result in death?

Washington Post reporter Wesley Lowery asked this after several highly publicized police killings of civilians in 2014. He found there were no federal statistics on the total. So, the Post began tracking these deaths on Jan. 1, 2015, for its Fatal Force project. The initiative collects data on such killings from local news reports, social media, law enforcement websites and police reports. It tracks a dozen pieces of data on each killing. According to The Post, 987 people were killed in 2017, 963 were killed in 2016, and 995 in 2015. About one fourth of the people killed in those years were found to be mentally ill.

66 How do these shootings compare by race?

According to the Fatal Force project, about 25 percent of the people killed by police in 2015-2017 were Black. They comprise about 13 percent of the U.S. population. Of civilians killed by police firearms in 2015-2017, about 17 percent were Hispanic or Latino. This is slightly less than their percentage in the population. Whites comprised about half the people killed in police shootings.

67 What is "non-escalation?"

Non-escalation and de-escalation are verbal tactics in the use-of-force continuum. Non-escalation is keeping a situation from getting out of hand. De-escalation is using techniques to bring a situation that is already out of hand to a manageable state. The Police Executive Research Forum published "30 Guiding Principles" in March 2016 that outlined de-escalation strategies. Some departments adopted the ideas. Other groups, including the Fraternal Order of Police and the International Association of Chiefs of Police, opposed it. They feared the strategy would cause dangerous hesitations. According to the 2017 Pew report, about one in four officers said they had no de-escalation training in the preceding year.

68 Why don't officers shoot to wound, rather than kill?

The objective is neither to wound nor to kill. The goal is to stop the threat. Aiming at the largest body mass increases the odds officers will hit their target and reduces the chance a stray shot will hit a bystander. The step below deadly force is less-lethal methods that hurt or discomfort suspects. Shooting to wound could jeopardize the safety of officers and others. David Klinger, professor of criminology and criminal justice at the University of Missouri-St. Louis, told ABC News that wounding would not stop life-threatening suspects. In such situations, he said, "deadly force is the appropriate response."

69 How do police feel about gun control?

According to Pew's 2017 study, 74 percent of officers said it is more important to protect gun ownership than to control it. However, the survey reported that 95 percent of officers favored laws preventing mentally ill people from buying guns. Most officers, 88 percent, said they favored mandatory background checks for private sales and gun shows. Six in 10 officers also favored a federal database to track all gun sales. Twenty-seven percent of male officers favored a ban on assault-style weapons. Fifty-seven percent of female officers did.

What percent of officers have discharged their service firearm while on duty, other than on a gun range or during training?

% who have not   **% who have**

72%	**All officers**	27%
70%	Men	30%
88%	Women	11%
69%	Whites	31%
79%	Blacks	21%
79%	Hispanics	20%

Statistics are taken from the Pew Research Center's 2017 report, "Behind the Badge."

Demographics

70 How many law enforcement officers are there in the United States?

According to the 2016 FBI Uniform Crime Reporting Project, there were 933,142 full-time law enforcement employees in the United States. Of those, 652,936 were officers. They were distributed across 13,160 departments. Men comprised 87.9 percent of the officers, whereas women comprised 60 percent of civilian employees. Historically low representation of women among uniformed employees is slowly improving.

71 Does the public show female officers less respect than male officers?

Pew's 2017 report asked officers in departments with more than 100 officers about this. Sixty percent of men and half of women said sexes were treated about the same. However, 43 percent of women said men were favored in assignments and promotion. Six percent of male officers agreed. Conversely, 33 percent of men said women were treated better and 6 percent of women agreed.

72 Do women and minority law enforcement officers face special challenges?

According to Pew, 60 percent of female officers reported verbal abuse by citizens during the previous month. That compares to 69 percent for men. About 70 percent of Hispanic and White police officers said they had experienced verbal abuse from the community in the prior month. Fifty-three percent of Black officers said so. Women were less likely to have struggled with suspects and far less likely to have fired a weapon in the line of duty.

73 Do female officers still have to do the same tasks when they get pregnant?

Pregnant officers can assume lower impact tasks. The federal Pregnancy Discrimination Act states "women affected by pregnancy, childbirth or related conditions" are to be treated the same "as other persons not so affected but similar in their ability or inability to work." The law covers all occupations.

74 Can transgender people become police?

Yes. Several cities reached out to transgender recruits after President Donald Trump tweeted they would be banned from the military in 2017. Welcoming cities included Austin, Houston, Cincinnati, San Diego and Seattle.

75 Are more officers politically conservative or liberal?

This is hard to pin down as officers see their personal politics as irrelevant to their mission. They are seldom surveyed about politics. However, app maker Verdant Labs analyzed Federal Election Commission data to see which way dozens of jobs leaned. There was not much difference in law enforcement. Among police officers, there were 51 Democrats for every 49 Republicans. Among police chiefs, there were 52 Democrats for every 48 Republicans. Sheriffs were 44 Democrats for every 56 Republicans. In the 2016 presidential election, The Fraternal Order of Police union, with more than 300,000 members, endorsed Donald Trump. The union has historically supported Republican candidates. The International Association of Chiefs of Police does not endorse presidential candidates.

Profiling

76 What is the difference between profiling and racial profiling?

Profiling can be a helpful method of recognizing potential criminal behavior. It judges individuals based on behavioral information or circumstances linking them to a suspected or potential crime. Racial profiling, which is to rely on race, rather than behavior or circumstances, is something different and is discouraged.

77 How does racial profiling happen?

Racial profiling is stopping, questioning, arresting or searching someone because of their perceived race or ethnicity. "Driving While Black," a Black person being in a predominantly White area, is not grounds for a stop. However, race can be one factor when police are looking for a suspect. Police say it can be impossible to know a person's race prior to stopping a car.

78 Do police show bias toward certain racial or ethnic groups?

A 2016 Stanford study of 60 million traffic stops in 20 states between 2011 and 2015 reported that Black drivers were stopped at a higher rate than White drivers. Latinos were stopped at a similar or lower rate. Black drivers pulled over for speeding were 20 percent more likely than Whites to be ticketed. Latino drivers were 30 percent more likely to get a ticket. Black and Latino drivers were about twice as likely as Whites to be searched. Furthermore, police searched Blacks and Latinos on the basis of far less evidence than Whites, the study said.

79 How often does racial profiling occur?

The Stanford study found "significant racial disparities in policing." In some areas, minorities are several times more likely than Whites to get stopped. The difficult part has been determining whether this is because of racial profiling. Other reasons for stops can be racial patterns in housing and employment. With traffic stops, for example, the places people live and the times they work or travel can increase their exposure to stops. A related issue is that Black and Hispanic people stopped for the same reason were more likely to get a ticket. The study said, "when pulled over for speeding, Black drivers are 20 percent more likely to get a ticket (rather than a warning) than White drivers, and Hispanic drivers are 30 percent more likely to be ticketed than White drivers."

80 Does body language play a role in profiling?

To a degree, yes. A person's inability to stay still, constant shrugging or head movements and flailing arms are clues outlined by police psychologist and forensic expert Greg Sancier, Ph.D. His checklist of behaviors is meant to help identify individuals on drugs or with potentially dangerous mental illnesses.

81 What is the role of local police in immigration issues?

This varies. For example, in 2012 the U.S. Supreme Court upheld Arizona legislation requiring officers to try to determine the immigration status of individuals they lawfully stop. Officers generally are prohibited from considering race or national origin beyond what is allowed under state and federal laws. The Washington State Patrol specifically limits how much officers can help federal immigration agents. According to the 2017 Pew Research report, Behind the Badge, 52 percent of officers said local law enforcement officers should identify undocumented immigrants. Forty-six percent said they should leave this mainly to federal officers.

Community Relations

82 What is community policing?

The U.S. Department of Justice describes community policing as emphasizing proactive rather than reactive procedures to prevent problems before they arise. Community policing considers complaints, concerns and potential danger to develop ways to reduce these issues. This is done through police outreach at schools, universities, churches and businesses.

83 How are community-police relations?

The 2017 study by the Pew Research Center found that most citizens rate police officers positively. However, there were large differences by age and race. The survey asked people to give police a rating of 0 to 100 on a "feeling thermometer," with 100 being warmest. Forty-eight percent of adults younger than 30 rated law enforcement warmly. Twenty-two percent were neutral and 29 percent were cold.

What are police relationships with races or ethnicities in their communities like?

% of officers that rate their relationship with Whites as excellent

White officers	92%
Black officers	91%
Hispanic officers	90%

% of officers that rate their relationship with Blacks as excellent

White officers	60%
Black officers	32%
Hispanic officers	60%

% of officers that rate their relationship with Hispanics as excellent

White officers	76%
Black officers	46%
Hispanic officers	71%

% of officers that rate their relationship with Asians as excellent

White officers	91%
Black officers	75%
Hispanic officers	88%

Statistics are taken from the Pew Research Center's 2017 report, "Behind the Badge."

What percent of officers are minorities? Has the percent increased?

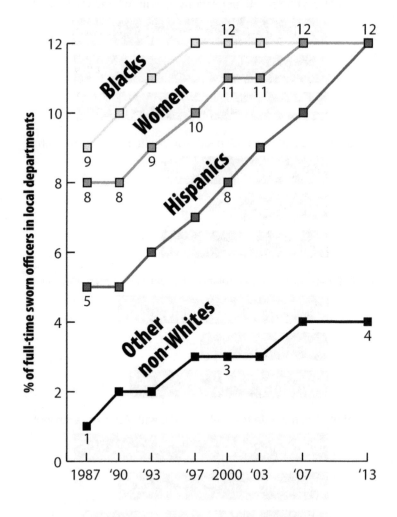

Statistics are taken from the Pew Research Center's 2017 report, "Behind the Badge."

What has happened in response to incidents with officers and Blacks?

% of officers reporting the following events have occurred in their department

☐ Departments with less than 300 officers
■ Departments with more than 2,600 officers

"Officers have become less willing to stop and question people who seem suspicious."

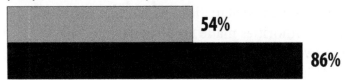

54%

86%

"Interactions between police and Blacks have become more tense."

61%

87%

"Officers have become more reluctant to use force when it is appropriate."

63%

85%

"Officers have become more concerned about their safety."

88%

95%

Statistics are taken from the Pew Research Center's 2017 report, "Behind the Badge."

Among people 65 and older, 80 percent rated police warmly, including 61 percent who said they have very warm views of officers. Seventy-four percent of White Americans gave law enforcement warm ratings, compared to 30 percent of Black Americans and 53 percent of Hispanics.

84 How diverse are law enforcement departments?

Bureau of Justice Statistics showed that racial and ethnic minorities made up 27 percent of full-time sworn personnel in state and local agencies in 2013. This was up from 25 percent in 2007 and 15 percent in 1987. Language skills, having lived in the community and gender are also important considerations.

85 Are racial tensions making police work more difficult?

Police say race-related protests, criticism and reforms have made their jobs harder. The Pew Research Center found that approximately three-quarters said colleagues are more reluctant to use appropriate force or to stop and question suspicious people. Some said racial tension has made them hesitant to follow protocols.

Have high-profile incidents with officers and Blacks made police work more difficult?

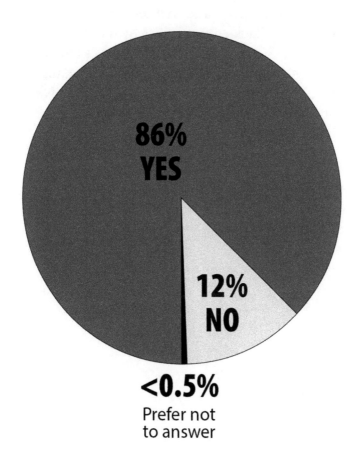

86%
YES

12%
NO

<0.5%
Prefer not
to answer

Statistics are taken from the Pew Research Center's 2017 report, "Behind the Badge."

86 What is the relationship between Black Lives Matter and police?

This does not have a simple answer. Both groups are stereotyped and misunderstood. Some Black officers support Black Lives Matter ideals. Those are "to build local power and to intervene in violence inflicted on Black communities by the state and vigilantes." Some news accounts, images and social media pit police and Black Lives Matter against each other. Yet officers sometimes protect Black Lives Matter members from counter-demonstrators. It is possible to support both groups.

Myths and Stereotypes

87 Is there a "blue wall of silence?"

Police and deputies swear to protect the community and civilians, and they also back up and help each other. When an officer is in trouble, the first person to help is almost always another officer. This contributes to the idea that a code of silence keeps officers from reporting each other's wrongdoing. This idea is behind a 1988 movie, "The Thin Blue Line," about a wrongful conviction. It is also true that many officers want to see bad cops brought to justice and that they initiate or lead investigations into corruption.

88 Do officers abuse their authority?

With more than 650,000 officers in the United States, it happens. Occasionally, top officials have been convicted. When it happens, other members of the department or law enforcement agencies expose or investigate it. Police and sheriffs' departments investigate and will suspend, fire or seek charges against officers who break the law. Self-enforcement also happens in other professions including doctors, lawyers, accountants and more.

89 Why do people joke about police and doughnuts?

Patrol officers, many of whom work 12-hour shifts, stop at doughnut shops because they open early and some stay open late. They always have coffee and bathrooms and are usually on busy streets that need policing. Doughnut shop owners like having officers present. Some departments organize community get-togethers over doughnuts and 5K/10K doughnut dashes for charity. When a historic bakery and doughnut shop in Clare, Michigan, faced closure, all nine members of the local police department took over. It is now called Cops and Doughnuts and has added locations, called precincts. A call there brought this explanation: "before the telephone, if people were in trouble or needed an officer, they would run to bakeries because they knew the officers would be there to help them." Not all police officers think doughnut jokes are funny.

90 What role do police play in parking enforcement?

Generally, not a big one. Police officers do have the authority to write parking tickets or order that vehicles be towed or impounded. But that work is usually handled by parking enforcers. Taking up a general parking issue with an officer can indicate a misunderstanding of what they do. In some communities, police and parking departments are in the same building and coordinate parking at special events.

91 Do police officers speed?

On-duty police officers are not allowed to speed or break driving laws except when necessary. Then, in accordance with policy and procedure, they must have their lights or siren on. If they speed while off duty, officers can be pulled over and ticketed, just like civilians.

92 Do journalists portray police accurately?

The Pew Research Center found that 81 percent of officers surveyed said media portrayals of police are unfair. Police impressions of media bias are linked to other feelings. Officers who feel strongly that the media portray them unfairly are more likely to say their work makes them frustrated and even angry. Though the feelings are related, Pew could not say whether one causes the other. Officers who feel mistreated by the media are more likely to say the public does not understand them.

93 Do TV shows portray police accurately?

Not really. Popular crime shows and movies dramatize or exaggerate the action and storylines to be more entertaining. TV cops shoot to wound or disarm bad guys. Recoils or wounds can be exaggerated (or muted). Less protection or equipment is worn, and crime-scene or DNA data comes back in an instant. Cases are wrapped up in 30 minutes or two hours. Even police reality shows are edited to condense action.

Equipment

94 What gear do officers carry on their belts?

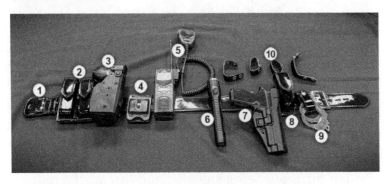

A patrol officer's belt: 1. A duty belt, sometimes called a Garrison belt or Sam Browne belt, which may hold as much as 15 pounds of gear 2. Magazine pouch with loaded ammunition clips 3. A Taser in its holster 4. Clip for police radio 5. Radio and microphone 6. Flashlight 7. Handgun, worn on the opposite side from the Taser 8. OC spray 9. Handcuffs 10. Belt keepers to secure the duty belt. The make of sidearm varies and officers might also carry an additional set of handcuffs or other items. Photo by Chelsea Aldrich, Michigan State University Police Department Operations Bureau.

95 What's inside a police car?

Onboard equipment: 1. Spotlights 2. Side lights show when turns are being signaled and display the red or blue lights. 3. Front-facing camera 4. Radar and control unit 5. Computer and keyboard (lid is down) 6. Camera monitor 7. Light and siren controller. Other equipment in the car includes a backseat camera, radio and microphone for talking with dispatchers, one or more equipment bags, first aid, tools or additional armored vests and weapons such as a shotgun or ArmaLite rifle. Photo by Michigan State University Police Officer Tim Mapley.

96 Do police have to be armed at all times?

Policies vary by agencies and among personnel within agencies. Even if it is not mandatory for officers to carry while off duty, many do for their own protection or to be prepared for the unexpected.

97 What is the debate about military-grade equipment?

This debate intensified after the 2014 Ferguson, Missouri, killing of Michael Brown. Videos showed police using surplus military equipment to quell street demonstrations. Some said the police looked like a paramilitary or occupying force and that this incited violence. In 2015, President Barack Obama banned the sale of some kinds of military equipment to local law enforcement agencies. In 2017, U.S. Attorney General Jeff Sessions said at an assembly of the Fraternal Order of Police that the government would roll that back. Much of this surplus equipment is non-military vehicles including mobile command centers, motorcycles, boats, helicopters, and protective equipment.

98 What kinds of less-lethal weapons do police use?

"Less-lethal" weapons are meant to incapacitate or immobilize. While they are less lethal than guns, they can still kill. Officers are trained on them and have protocols for deciding appropriate use. The National Institute of Justice lists seven types of weapons:

- Conducted-energy devices such as stun guns (including Tasers) and stun belts, which induce involuntary muscle contractions
- Directed energy devices, which radiate energy that feels like blunt force
- Chemicals, including OC spray, or oleoresin capsicum, better known as pepper spray, tear gas and stink bombs
- Distractors that incapacitate with bright lights or noise, and the laser dazzler
- Vehicle-stopping equipment such as spike strips used to stop fleeing cars
- Barriers including nets, foam and physical barriers
- Blunt-force projectiles such as batons and bean bag guns

99 Why and how do police use body-worn cameras?

Officers wear cameras to record evidence and show how they did their work. They tend to wear the camera in the center of their chest for the best field of view. Pew research showed that civilians were more favorable about the body-worn cameras than police. Civilians more often said body-worn cameras make people cooperate and police act more appropriately.

100 How has the digital age affected police work?

Police now have access to larger databases. They can communicate better and analyze data faster. Technology has improved their protective clothing and gear and has given them computer simulations for weapons training. However, it has also brought continued challenges in cybercrime.

What to do in a traffic stop

There are tens of millions of traffic stops every year. They cause anxiety for motorists and for police. Every month, stops have tragic results, such as assaults or fatal accidents. Officers receive training on how to handle traffic stops and are on high alert when they make them. Few motorists are as prepared. Recently, several states have passed legislation requiring drivers to be trained on how to respond in a traffic stop. These guidelines come from several sources. They include the Michigan State University Police Department, the State of Illinois Secretary of State, the Michigan Sheriffs' Association and the Roseville (Michigan) Police Department.

Why do officers stop drivers?

- Suspicion of a traffic violation or other crime
- Violations such as a burned-out headlight or expired registration tag
- If someone seems to need help
- If someone fits the description of a suspect
- To seek information about a crime

What should drivers do?

- If an officer turns on the siren or is flashing the lights, slow down. Pull off to the right, or into someplace safe like a side street or parking lot. Keep the lights on. Officers might park at an angle behind you to protect themselves from approaching vehicles. If you are driving past a traffic stop, move at least one lane over from the patrol car or, if you can't change lanes safely, slow down. In most states, this is the law.
- If you feel unsafe or believe you are being stopped by an impostor, turn on the emergency flashers and drive slowly to the closest well-lit location, such as a store or gas station. If still unsure, call 911 and report what is happening.
- At night, turn on the interior light.
- Stay calm. Wait.
- Keep your hands where they can be seen. High on the steering wheel is best.
- Ask passengers to sit still and keep their hands visible, too.
- The officer may stand slightly behind the driver or passenger side door and might use a flashlight. This can seem awkward or intimidating, but is done for the officer's safety.
- Do not get out of the vehicle unless asked. Then, follow instructions.
- The officer is likely to ask for your driver's license, vehicle registration and proof of insurance. Do not get them until asked. Then, tell the officer where they are before reaching for them.

- If you have a concealed pistol license and your firearm is on your person or in the passenger compartment, inform the officer and ask them how they would like you to proceed. If you have a CPL and you do not have a firearm, it may not be mandatory in your state to disclose that you have a CPL. Do not reach for anything unless told to.
- Do not try to touch an officer. This can seem threatening.
- If the officer has not said why you were stopped, now is the time to ask.
- If you think the ticket is unjust, plan to challenge it in court, not on the side of the road. The ticket does not make you guilty of anything and it will say how you can challenge it.
- Speak to officers with the courtesy you expect from them.
- Cooperation can save time. A conflict at this moment can make things worse.

May I record the traffic stop?

- Yes. But don't alarm officers by holding a metallic object in your hand until they know what it is.
- An officer who believes a video or audio contains evidence is allowed to seize it.

Can officers search drivers, passengers or the vehicle?

- If they receive permission from the people in the vehicle, yes.
- You can be searched without permission if you are being arrested, if there is a search warrant or if the officer has a reasonable belief that you have committed a crime, or plan to. Another reason is if the officer believes there is evidence in the vehicle.
- You could be frisked if the officer believes you may be armed.

What if I am arrested and questioned?

- Follow instructions. Resistance can result in greater force.
- Be honest. Lying about a serious crime may have serious legal consequences.
- You have the right to remain silent and anything you say can be used against you in court.
- Officers are not required to advise suspects of their rights to remain silent immediately upon arrest.
- If taken in for questioning you have the right to have a lawyer present while being questioned.
- If you cannot afford to hire a lawyer, one will be appointed at no cost.

- Phone calls after arrest are not a right. They may be allowed, however.

What if I think I was treated unprofessionally?

- Debating the officer seldom helps and can make things worse. The courtroom is the place for disagreements.
- Contact the officer's immediate supervisor or watch commnder. If you are not satisfied, you may file a formal complaint.

Another resource is "Lights in the Mirror," a 15-minute video collaboration by the Illinois State Police, Illinois Sheriffs' Association, the Illinois Association of Chiefs of Police and the FBI Springfield Division. See video at: https://www.youtube.com/watch?v=0nCUvvozkIE

Police jargon

Many occupational groups use jargon that saves time and reflects their shared responsibilities and experiences. Law enforcement is no exception. Acronyms replace names for equipment or phrases, and numbers can refer to laws or forms. The amount of conversation carried by radio makes verbal shorthand necessary, and some police talk is borrowed from military communication. The military alphabet, beginning with Alpha, Bravo, Charlie, is used for initials of some terms. Police slang has hundreds of terms and many terms mean more than one thing. Given that so much of law enforcement is organized at the local level, many terms vary by jurisdiction or region. Few terms are universal, so a dictionary of police jargon would be unlikely to match any community. This is a partial list of terms used just for police cars, which also have varied styles and uses.

- Adam unit: one officer in car
- Black and white
- Blue and white
- Boston unit: two officers in car
- Bubblegum machine
- Cherry top
- Civic cruiser
- Cop car
- Cruiser
- Five-0

- Fuzzmobile
- Ghost car: unmarked police car
- Panda car
- Patrol car
- Police cruiser
- Police interceptor
- Police vehicle
- Prowl car
- Rollers
- Slick top
- Squad car
- Whale

10 codes or signal codes: These are shorthand, usually used over the radio, as time-savers for often-used phrases. Police are not the only ones who use them. You might have heard of "10-4," which means "I understand that transmission," or "10-20," which means location. Sometimes, 10 codes help police communicate without alerting civilians or suspects to what they are talking about. Some departments do not use 10 codes and have adopted code responses or signal codes. They work in similar fashion, but begin with the word "code" or "signal" followed by a number. The reason for the word before the number is that with early equipment the first word or syllable might be cut off. Using a word before the number lets the important information get through. Not all departments assign the same meanings to all codes. When the ABC police drama "Detroit 1-8-7" aired, it caught flack because 187 does not mean murder under Michigan law. That is murder's number under the California Penal Code.

Police funeral etiquette

Funerals are a time-honored way for law enforcement officers to recognize comrades and to reflect on their own careers. There is a solidarity among first responders, so officers from miles away might be designated to attend a funeral to convey their own respects and those of their departments. Some police funerals attract public attention for their size or for the line-of-duty circumstances that led to them. Still, they are solemn, sacred occasions with personal significance that can make them emotionally difficult to attend. While these funerals are tributes to the officers and meant to be a comfort to their families, they are not intended as spectacles. Processions can delay motorists, but this inconvenience is tiny compared to the sacrifices expected of officers.

There is no universal script or procedure for funerals. Each officer and family is different, as are the circumstances and the department they served in. These lead to variations, but some traditions and protocols are frequently observed at funerals for police, firefighters and the military.

One consideration in the formality and scope of a police funeral is the position the person held and the circumstances of the death. There are differences based on whether the death was in the line of duty, whether the person was an officer or a civilian employee, whether they were active-duty or retired or separated, and there are customs for family members.

K-9s face the same risks as their human partners and can receive police funerals, too. Like human members of the force, they leave partners behind and the funeral can help others recognize and process the loss.

The most formal funerals are for line-of-duty deaths. Elements can include:

- Casket watch or vigil
- Full military-style honors
- Color (flag) guard
- Members of the honor guard keep their hats on during the service while others remove them, except to deliver a final salute.
- There is often an invocation, prayer and eulogy.
- Speakers may be from the department, union, government or family.
- Usually at the cemetery there is a salute of 21 bells or three rifle volleys.
- A bagpiper might play "Amazing Grace."
- Final radio call, "End of Watch," is also at the cemetery. This tradition has a dispatcher calling the officer by badge number and then reporting that there is no response. The call might note the length of service and the time and date and conclude with "Gone, but not forgotten" or "Rest in peace." Frequently, the badge number of a fallen officer is retired.

Organizations

FBI Uniform Crime Reporting Program,
https://ucr.fbi.gov

Federal Law Enforcement Training Centers,
https://fletc.gov

Fraternal Order of Police, https://fop.net

Hispanic American Police Command Officers
Association, https://hapcoa.org

Hispanic Police Officers Association,
https://hpoadade.org

International Association of Campus Law Enforcement
Administrators, https://iaclea.org

International Association of Chiefs of Police,
https://theiacp.org

International Association of Chiefs of Police job board,
https://discoverpolicing.org

International Association of Directors of Law
Enforcement Standards and Training,
https://iadlest.org

International Association of Women Police,
https://iawp.org/about.htm

International Law Enforcement Educators and Trainers
Association, https://Ileeta.org

International Union of Police Associations,
https://iupa.org

Major Cities Chiefs Association,
https://majorcitieschiefs.com/members.php

Michigan Association of Chiefs of Police,
https://michiganpolicechiefs.org

Michigan Commission on Law Enforcement Standards,
https://michigan.gov/mcoles

Michigan Sheriffs' Association,
https://misheriff.org

National Academy of Sciences' Committee on Law and
Justice,
https://sites.nationalacademies.org/DBASSE/CLAJ/
index.htm

National Asian Peace Officers Association,
https://napoablue.org

National Association of Black Law Enforcement
Officers, Inc.,
https://nableo.org

National Association of Chiefs of Police,
https://nacoponline.org

National Association of Police Organizations,
https://napo.org

National Association of Women Law Enforcement
Executives, https://nawlee.org/about-us/mission

National Black Police Association,
https://blackpolice.org

National Center for Campus Public Safety,
https://nccpsafety.org

National Criminal Justice Reference Service,
https://ncjrs.gov

National Latino Peace Officers Association,
https://nlpoa.com/?page=about_us

National Law Enforcement Officers Memorial Fund, https://nleomf.com

National Organization of Black Law Enforcement Executives, https://noblenational.org

National Police Research Platform, https://uicclj.squarespace.com

National Sheriffs' Association, https://sheriffs.org

The National Native American Law Enforcement Association, https://nnalea.org

Research

Bureau of Justice Statistics, https://bjs.gov

The U.S. government's "primary source for criminal justice statistics." Its mission is "to collect, analyze, publish, and disseminate information on crime, criminal offenders, victims of crime, and the operation of justice systems at all levels of government." It is part of the U.S. Department of Justice.

Police Executive Research Forum, https://policeforum.org

"An independent research organization that focuses on critical issues in policing." Identifies, "best practices on fundamental issues such as reducing police use of force; developing community policing and problem-oriented policing; using technologies to deliver police services to the community; and evaluating crime reduction strategies."

Police Section of the Academy of Criminal Justice Sciences, https://acjs.org

Promotes "criminal justice education, research, and policy analysis ... for both educators and practitioners."

The previous two organizations are associated with Police Quarterly, a peer-reviewed journal with empirical studies related to policing. It publishes qualitative and quantitative articles that emphasize policy-oriented research.

Governing the States and Localities, https://governing.com

This magazine publishes articles about issues such as staffing, overtime, diversity, community policing and more. The search option on its home page helps find these.

Pew Research Center, http://www.pewsocialtrends.org/2017/01/11/behind-the-badge/

This link will take you to its survey of nearly 8,000 officers, conducted by the National Police Research Platform. The platform is at http://uicclj.squarespace.com/

The National Police Suicide Foundation, https://www.psf.org

It was founded in 1997 to combat the increasing number of suicides by law enforcement officers. It has added emergency responders to its mission.

Epilogue

This guide, like all the guides in this series, is just a starting point. It is meant to replace stereotypes with accurate information. But studies and statistics are no substitute for really getting to know people. Law enforcement officers live in and serve every community in the United States. Most are willing to talk about their work, why they do it and the challenges it brings. While a traffic stop is not the best place for a conversation, there are plenty of others. Departments have open houses, community events and citizen councils. All are places to get to know police officers, sheriff's deputies and other local law enforcers better. We recommend you take those opportunities, and ask the questions you would still like answers to after reading this guide, to develop a mutual and constructive understanding. Thank you.

Our Story

The 100 Questions and Answers series springs from the idea that good journalism should increase cross-cultural competence and understanding. Most of our guides are created by Michigan State University journalism students.

We use journalistic interviews to surface the simple, everyday questions that people have about each other but might be afraid to ask. We use research and reporting to get the answers and then put them where people can find them, read them and learn about each other.

These cultural competence guides are meant to be conversation starters. We want people to use these guides to get some baseline understanding and to feel comfortable asking more questions. We put a resources section in every guide we make and we arrange community conversations. While the guides can answer questions in private, they are meant to spark discussions.

Making these has taught us that people are not that different from each other. People share more similarities than differences. We all want the same things for ourselves and for our families. We want to be accepted, respected and understood.

Please email your thoughts and suggestions to Series Editor Joe Grimm at joe.grimm@gmail.com, at the Michigan State University School of Journalism.

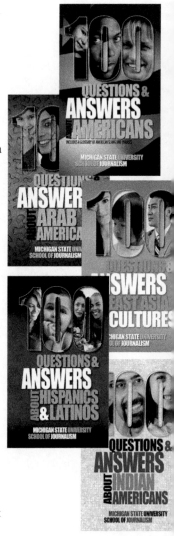

Related Books

100 Questions and Answers About Americans
Michigan State University School of Journalism, 2013
This guide answers some of the first questions asked by
newcomers to the United States. Questions represent
dozens of nationalities coming from Africa, Asia,
Australia, Europe and North and South America. Good
for international students, guests and new immigrants.
http://news.jrn.msu.edu/culturalcompetence/

ISBN: 978-1-939880-20-8

100 Questions and Answers About Arab Americans
Michigan State University School of Journalism, 2014
The terror attacks of Sept. 11, 2001, propelled these Americans into a difficult position where they are victimized
twice. The guide addresses stereotypes, bias and misin-
formation. Key subjects are origins, religion, language
and customs. A map shows places of national origin.
http://news.jrn.msu.edu/culturalcompetence/

ISBN: 978-1-939880-56-7

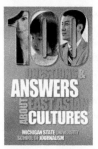

100 Questions and Answers About East Asian Cultures
Michigan State University School of Journalism, 2014
Large university enrollments from Asia prompted
this guide as an aid for understanding cultural differences. The focus is on people from China, Japan,
Korea and Taiwan and includes Mongolia, Hong
Kong and Macau. The guide includes history, language, values, religion, foods and more.
http://news.jrn.msu.edu/culturalcompetence/

ISBN: 978-939880-50-5

100 Questions and Answers About Hispanics & Latinos
Michigan State University School of Journalism, 2014
This group became the largest ethnic minority in the
United States in 2014 and this guide answers many of
the basic questions about it. Questions were suggested
by Hispanics and Latinos. Includes maps and charts
on origin and size of various Hispanic populations.
http://news.jrn.msu.edu/culturalcompetence/

ISBN: 978-1-939880-44-4

Print and ebooks available on Amazon.com and other retailers.

Related Books

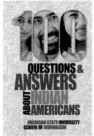

100 Questions and Answers About Indian Americans
Michigan State University School of Journalism, 2013
In answering questions about Indian Americans, this guide also addresses Pakistanis, Bangladeshis and others from South Asia. The guide covers religion, issues of history, colonization and national partitioning, offshoring and immigration, income, education, language and family.
http://news.jrn.msu.edu/culturalcompetence/

ISBN: 978-1-939880-00-0 m

100 Questions, 500 Nations: A Guide to Native America
Michigan State University School of Journalism, 2014
This guide was created in partnership with the Native American Journalists Association. The guide covers tribal sovereignty, treaties and gaming, in addition to answers about population, religion, U.S. policies and politics. The guide includes the list of federally recognized tribes.
http://news.jrn.msu.edu/culturalcompetence/

ISBN: 978-1-939880-38-3

100 Questions and Answers About Veterans
Michigan State University School of Journalism, 2015
This guide treats the more than 20 million U.S. military veterans as a cultural group with distinctive training, experiences and jargon. Graphics depict attitudes, adjustment challenges, rank, income and demographics. Includes six video interviews by Detroit Public Television.
http://news.jrn.msu.edu/culturalcompetence/

ISBN: 978-1-942011-00-2

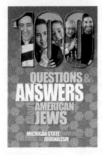

100 Questions and Answers About American Jews
Michigan State University School of Journalism 2016
We begin by asking and answering what it means to be Jewish in America. The answers to these wide-ranging, base-level questions will ground most people and set them up for meaningful conversations with Jewish acquaintances.
http://news.jrn.msu.edu/culturalcompetence/

ISBN: 978-1-942011-22-4

Print and ebooks available on Amazon.com and other retailers.

Related Books

100 Questions and Answers About Muslim Americans
Michigan State University School of Journalism, 2014
This guide was done at a time of rising intolerance in
the United States toward Muslims. The guide describes
the presence of this religious group around the world
and inside the United States. It includes audio on
how to pronounce some basic Muslim words.
http://news.jrn.msu.edu/culturalcompetence/

ISBN: 978-1-939880-79-6

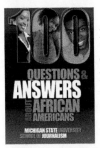

100 Questions and Answers About African Americans
Michigan State University School of Journalism, 2016
Learn about the racial issues that W.E.B. DuBois said in
1900 would be the big challenge for the 20th century.
This guide explores Black and African American identity,
history, language, contributions and more. Learn more
about current issues in American cities and campuses.
http://news.jrn.msu.edu/culturalcompetence/

ISBN: 978-1-942011-19-4

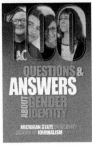

100 Questions and Answers About Immigrants to the U.S.
Michigan State University School of Journalism 2016
This simple, introductory guide answers 100 of the
basic questions people ask about U.S. immigrants
and immigration in everyday conversation. It
has answers about identity, language, religion,
culture, customs, social norms, economics,
politics, education, work, families and food.

ISBN: 978-1-934879-63-4

100 Questions and Answers about Gender Identity
Michigan State University School of Journalism 2017
This simple, introductory guide answers 100 of
the basic questions people ask about transgender
people in everyday conversation. The questions
come from interviews with transgender people
who say these are issues they frequently get asked
about or wish people knew more about.

ISBN: 978-1-64180-002-0

Print and ebooks available on Amazon.com and other retailers.